In loving memory of

_____

_____

_____

_____

NAME   COMMENT

NAME   COMMENT

NAME   COMMENT

NAME   COMMENT

NAME   COMMENT

NAME   COMMENT

NAME   COMMENT

NAME   COMMENT

NAME   COMMENT

NAME   COMMENT

NAME   COMMENT

NAME   COMMENT

NAME COMMENT

www.ingramcontent.com/pod-product-compliance
Lightning Source LLC
Chambersburg PA
CBHW041608260326
41914CB00012B/1424